Medical Malpractice: Case Study on New York: HRD-87-21S-5

U.S. Government Accountability Office (GAO)

The BiblioGov Project is an effort to expand awareness of the public documents and records of the U.S. Government via print publications. In broadening the public understanding of government and its work, an enlightened democracy can grow and prosper. Ranging from historic Congressional Bills to the most recent Budget of the United States Government, the BiblioGov Project spans a wealth of government information. These works are now made available through an environmentally friendly, print-on-demand basis, using only what is necessary to meet the required demands of an interested public. We invite you to learn of the records of the U.S. Government, heightening the knowledge and debate that can lead from such publications.

Included are the following Collections:

Budget of The United States Government
Presidential Documents
United States Code
Education Reports from ERIC
GAO Reports
History of Bills
House Rules and Manual
Public and Private Laws

Code of Federal Regulations
Congressional Documents
Economic Indicators
Federal Register
Government Manuals
House Journal
Privacy act Issuances
Statutes at Large

December 1986

MEDICAL MALPRACTICE

Case Study on New York

537698

HRD-87-21S-5

Preface

December 31, 1986

Representative John Edward Porter and Senator John Heinz, Chairman, Senate Special Committee on Aging, asked GAO to identify the actions taken by the states to address medical malpractice insurance problems and to determine changes in insurance costs, the number of claims filed, and the average amount paid per claim. These case studies discuss the situation in each state.

This study on New York focuses on the views of various interest groups on perceived problems, actions taken by the states to deal with the problems, the results of these actions, and the need for federal involvement. A summary of the findings for all six case studies can be found in our overall report, <u>Medical Malpractice: Six State Case Studies Show Claims and Insurance Costs Still Rise Despite Reforms</u> (GAO/HRD-87-21, December 31, 1986).

Richard L. Fogel

Richard L. Fogel
Assistant Comptroller General
for Human Resources Programs

Overview

New York's medical malpractice insurance crisis in the mid-1970's was one of availability, due largely to the withdrawal of two of the larger insurers in the state. By the 1980's, the problem shifted to one of affordability as companies raised their rates. The New York state legislature responded to malpractice problems by various legislative initiatives passed in 1975, 1976, 1981, 1985, and 1986. Although it is too early to tell how effective the 1985 and 1986 reforms will be, insurance rates have continued to climb for hospitals and physicians, particularly for high-risk specialties. The rates are among the highest in the nation.

As of January 1, 1986, the rates of New York's leading physician insurer were generally higher in the New York City area than in the rest of the state.

In 1984, the average paid claim against New York physicians was also considerably higher than the St. Paul Company's national average—$104,810 versus $56,739. Similarly, the average paid claim in 1984 against New York hospitals was $88,917 compared with the St. Paul Company's national average of $30,279.

Of the interest groups surveyed, New York's Hospital Association, Bar Association, and the Trial Lawyers Association supported additional actions to strengthen licensing and relicensing of physicians. To police the profession, the New York Bar Association favored setting insurance rates for physicians according to their malpractice claims and loss experiences rather than revoking physician licenses.

There was no agreement among the interest groups surveyed that the federal government should assume a role in addressing medical malpractice insurance problems. Only the physician group supported a federal role to develop a uniform system for resolving medical malpractice claims.

Contents

Figures

Chapter 1

New York: Claims and Premiums Are High but Recent State Reforms May Help

Background

Population, Physician, and Hospital Characteristics

New York is the second most populous state. About 85 percent of its 17.7 million people live in urban areas.[1] New York had 56,392 physicians as of December 31, 1985,[2] and 263 nonfederal community hospitals with 79,912 available beds in 1984.[3] A total of 44,732 physicians were providing patient care—29,118 were office-based and 15,614 were hospital-based. Table 1 shows the distribution of patient care physicians among 13 selected specialties:

Table 1: Number of Nonfederal Patient Care Physicians in New York in Selected Specialties as of December 31, 1985

	Office-based practice	Hospital-based practice		Total
		Residents	Full-time physician staff	
General practice	2,829	355	225	3,409
Internal medicine	6,073	2,993	898	9,964
Pediatrics	2,338	963	494	3,795
Psychiatry	2,612	784	1,068	4,464
Pathology	379	315	415	1,109
Radiology	524	41	275	840
Ophthalmology	1,224	203	45	1,472
General surgery	2,213	1,383	271	3,867
Anesthesiology	1,270	494	220	1,984
Plastic surgery	331	39	21	391
Orthopedic surgery	921	325	66	1,312
Obstetrics/gynecology	2,075	611	220	2,906
Neurosurgery	176	67	24	267

Of the 263 community hospitals, 208 are nongovernment, not-for-profit; 32 are state and local government; and 23 are investor-owned (for-profit). Seventy-eight percent of the state's hospital beds were in nongovernment, not-for-profit hospitals; 16 percent were in state and local government hospitals, and 6 percent were in investor-owned hospitals. The most common community hospital sizes are the 100- to 199-bed

---

[1]Population and ranking are as of July 1, 1984 (preliminary), and the urban/rural mix is as of April 1, 1980, from the Statistical Abstract of the United States, 1986, 106th Edition, pp. 10, 12.

[2]Physician Characteristics and Distribution in the U.S., 1986 Edition, Department of Data Release Services, Division of Survey of Data Resources, American Medical Association (forthcoming).

[3]Hospital Statistics, 1985 Edition, American Hospital Association, p. 106.

and 200- to 299-bed facilities with 58 and 56 such hospitals, respectively. These hospitals account for 28 percent of the state's hospital beds. New York has 42 hospitals with 500 beds or more each, which account for 42 percent of the community hospital beds. The occupancy rate of the community hospitals was 87 percent in 1984.

Regulation of Insurance Rates and Description of Medical Malpractice Insurers

New York is a "prior approval" state. Insurance companies must file a proposed rate change with the state insurance department and receive approval before they can change the rate. Rates are required to not be unreasonable, discriminatory, or inadequate. The state insurance department requires the Medical Malpractice Insurance Association, a Joint Underwriting Association, to set the lowest rate possible to remain solvent. The insurance department also requires all companies to file annual statements, submit a formal plan of operation, and receive a tri-annual examination.

Medical Liability Mutual Insurance Company, a physician-owned company, is the leading insurer in New York's physician medical malpractice insurance market. According to company officials, the company has about 70 percent of the market.

The leading insurer of hospitals is the Hospital Underwriters Mutual Insurance Company, which, as of January 1, 1985, insured 106 hospitals, or about 40 percent of the community hospitals in the state.

Insurance companies providing malpractice insurance coverage in New York use from one to five rating territories. The predominately written coverage limits for both New York physician and hospital malpractice policies were $1 million/$3 million.

Since 1975, the Medical Malpractice Insurance Association and the Medical Liability Mutual Insurance Company have requested approval of malpractice rate increases a number of times. In 1980, for example, the former requested an increase of 186 percent, but 24 percent was approved. The same rate was also approved for the latter company. The state insurance department granted further increases of 32 percent for 1984, 14 percent for 1985, and 9 percent for 1986.

Medical Malpractice Situation in the Mid-1970's

Availability of medical malpractice insurance in the mid-1970's was a major problem in New York. Before 1975, Employers Mutual of Wausau had been the leading malpractice insurer for physicians and hospitals in New York. In July 1974, Wausau withdrew from the malpractice market because it had become unprofitable due to an increase in malpractice suits and the size of awards. To fill this void, Argonaut Insurance Company of California entered the market in 1974 with an initial rate exceeding Wausau's by 94 percent. Argonaut announced an increase of 197 percent and then announced its withdrawal from the New York physician insurance market effective July 1, 1975.

Response to Problems

The New York state legislature enacted numerous reforms between 1974 and 1986 to deal with the state's malpractice insurance problem. Major provisions were as follows:

1974

- Created pretrial screening and mediation panels for all malpractice suits.

1975

- Reduced statute of limitations for reporting malpractice claims from 3 to 2-1/2 years.
- Required insurers to report claims information to the Superintendent of Insurance.
- Limited applicability of doctrine of informed consent.
- Provided that evidence concerning payments from collateral sources can be presented to a jury concerning plaintiff's payments from such sources as insurance, social security, workers' compensation, or other employee benefits.
- Provided that a malpractice panel's recommendations were admissible if three members concur on the question of liability. The panel recommendation shall not be binding on the jury or court.
- Created a board for professional medical conduct to investigate and conduct hearings.

1976

- Required itemized verdict in medical malpractice actions. The jury will specify the amount assigned to but not limited to medical expenses, loss of earnings, impairment of earning ability, and pain and suffering.

- Provided that contingent fees for attorneys will not exceed the amount of compensation provided for in either of the following schedules—50 percent of the first $1,000; 40 percent of the next $2,000; 35 percent of the next $22,000; and 25 percent of any amount over $25,000; or 33-1/3 percent of the sum recovered.
- Provided that in an action for medical malpractice, the plaintiff should not state the amount of damages sought.

1985

- Increased malpractice prevention programs.
- Provided for full disclosure of the qualifications of expert witnesses and the substance of the testimony presented.
- Required a conference before going to court to encourage settlement, simplify or limit issues, and establish a timetable for disclosure.
- Required that any award be reduced by other sources of insurance payable in the future.
- Limited the lump-sum payment of judgments for future damages to $250,000. For pain and suffering, the payment period is limited to a maximum of 10 years.
- Allows a court to award attorney's fees and court costs up to $10,000 in cases involving frivolous actions or defenses.
- Reduced contingency fees for plaintiffs' attorneys. The fee schedule is 30 percent of the first $250,000; 25 percent of the next $250,000; 20 percent of the next $500,000; 15 percent of the next $250,000; and 10 percent of any further amount.
- Required insurers to offer additional coverage of $1 million/$3 million over and above the $1 million/$3 million coverage presently offered.
- Required that amounts awarded by a jury or court be itemized between past and future damages.

The legislation also directed the Superintendent of Insurance to review premiums for the 1984/1985 premium year and reduce rates due to the tort reforms enacted. This resulted in a mandated rate rollback of 15 percent for individual physicians' malpractice policies.

1986

- Modified the doctrine of joint and several liability in personal injury cases. In cases involving jointly liable defendants where the liability of the individual defendant is found to be 50 percent or less of the total liability, that defendant's liability for the "noneconomic loss" portion of an award shall not exceed that defendant's equitable share of the negligence.

- Required reporting and investigation of hospital-based malpractice incidents.
- Required that all medical malpractice insurance policies for primary levels of coverage must be issued or renewed solely on a claims-made basis, except occurrence policies must be renewed for (1) physicians who already have and elect to continue such coverage and (2) physicians who are 60 years old or older as of July 1, 1986 and elect such coverage.
- Required insurers to file quarterly reports with the Superintendent of Insurance and the Commissioner of Health on all medical malpractice claims, policy cancellations, and provider rate adjustments.
- Expanded the authority of the Superintendent of Insurance to set and review insurance rates and monitor the need for rate increases.
- Permitted arbitration of damages under certain conditions.
- Strengthened and expanded the activities of the board for professional medical conduct. In certain circumstances, physicians can be placed on probation and have their practices monitored by other physicians, including review of patient records and bills.

Effect of New York Tort Reforms

No specific tort reforms were identified by three or more of the interest groups we surveyed in New York as having had any major effect.[4] Five of the six interest groups agreed that it was too soon to determine any effect from the changes resulting from the 1985 legislation. Comments were not solicited on the most recent state legislation passed in July 1986.

Key Indicators of the Situation Since 1980

As the 1980's progressed, New York's medical malpractice insurance problem became less one of availability and increasingly one of affordability. The Medical Liability Mutual Insurance Company's increases in the cost of malpractice insurance ranged from 96 percent for anesthesiology to 355 percent for pathology and psychiatry during the period 1980-86. Premiums of the largest hospital insurer remained unchanged until 1986, when they increased by 32 percent.

---

[4]Our methodology for obtaining the views of major interest groups and for analyzing their responses is described in GAO/HRD-87-21, pp. 10-11. The specific interest groups for New York are presented in appendix II of this report.

From 1980 to 1984, the frequency of claims per 100 physicians increased 32 percent, and the size of paid claims increased dramatically. During the same period, the number of claims against hospitals increased, but the size of claims paid against hospitals remained relatively unchanged.

Physicians

Cost of Malpractice Insurance

Cost of malpractice insurance for New York physicians varies by specialty and location of practice within the state. The rates for physicians practicing in and around the New York City area insured by the Medical Liability Mutual Insurance Company are higher than the rates paid by physicians practicing outside that area. For example, as of January 1, 1986, a neurosurgeon practicing in Nassau and Suffolk County would pay $95,084 for a $1 million/$3 million policy, while the same neurosurgeon practicing outside the New York City area would pay $43,019 for the same coverage. Further, the premium costs vary significantly among different specialties in the same area.

The rate of increase in malpractice insurance costs has not been uniform among the specialties. As shown in table 2, the increases in Medical Mutual's rates from 1980 to 1986 range from 96 percent for anesthesiology to 355 percent for psychiatry. The median increase was 307 percent.

Table 2: Cost of Insurance[a] for Selected Specialties, 1980 and 1986

Specialty	1980	1986	Percent increase 1980-86
General practice (no surgery)	$1,361	4,818	254
Internal medicine (no surgery)	1,698	6,919	307
Pediatrics	1,698	6,919	307
Pathology	679	3,086	354
General practice (minor surgery)	2,120	9,220	335
Internal medicine (minor surgery)	1,698	7,233	326
Radiology	1,698	6,919	307
Psychiatry	2,120	9,642	355
Ophthalmology/surgery	3,006	7,233	141
General surgery	7,519	20,642	175
Anesthesiology	6,933	13,598	96
Plastic surgery	6,933	25,642	270
Orthopedic/surgery	11,538	36,472	216
Obstetrics/gynecology	7,894	35,133	345
Neurosurgery	11,538	43,019	273

[a]Rates shown are those of Medical Liability Mutual Insurance Company for a $1 million/$3 million occurrence policy as of January 1 each year in the rating territory outside the New York metropolitan area, where the largest number of physicians are insured. Under an occurrence policy, the insurance company is liable for any incidents that occurred during the period the policy was in force, regardless of when the claim may be filed.

Frequency of Claims

The combined claims experience for five insurers of New York physicians indicated that the frequency of claims filed per 100 physicians remained relatively stable from 1980 to 1984. However, this frequency of claims may not be fully representative of the situation in New York because three of the five companies from which we collected data only began writing malpractice insurance in the state since 1981. According to our consulting actuary, the frequency of claims filed against these three companies does not reflect the experience one would expect had they been writing insurance in the state for a longer period since it takes a number of years for claims to be filed. Consequently, the frequency of claims for these companies may be understated. To illustrate this difference, in 1984 the frequency of claims filed against the Medical Liability Mutual Insurance Company, a company writing insurance in New York since 1975, was 35.7 claims per 100 physicians, whereas the frequency of claims filed against the other three companies was 4.4 per 100 physicians. We believe that the data we obtained from the Medical Liability Mutual Insurance Company best illustrate the frequency of claims for physicians in New York. The frequency of claims for this company,

which insures about 70 percent of the market, increased from 27.1 to
35.7 claims per 100 physicians between 1980 and 1984—an increase of
32 percent, as shown in figure 1.

Figure 1: Frequency of Claims per 100 Physicians Insured by The Medical Liability Mutual Insurance Company, 1980-84

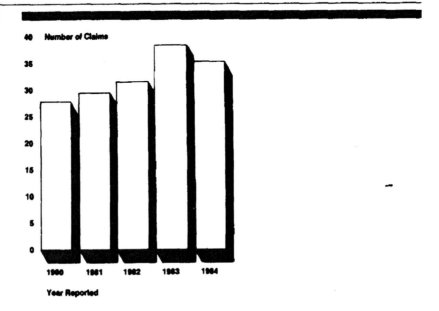

We did not compute the frequency of claims for each of the selected
specialties because of limitations in the data provided by the New York
insurers.

Size of Awards and Settlements

The combined data shown in figure 2 indicate that the average paid
claim increased significantly over the period from 1980 to 1984.[5]

---

[5]Since the Medical Liability Mutual Insurance Company began insuring physicians in 1975, some of
this growth in the average paid claim can be attributed to the normal expected insurance claim
payout pattern.

**Figure 2: Average Paid Claim for
Physicians, 1980-84**

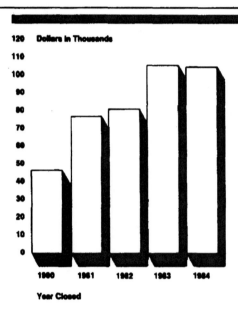

We did not compute the average paid claim for each selected specialty
because of limitations in the data provided by the New York insurers.

Cost to Investigate and Defend
Claims

Combined data from the New York insurers shows that the average cost
to investigate and defend claims against New York physicians increased
from $3,822 in 1980 to $10,063 in 1984—an increase of 163 percent.

In 1980, 36 percent of the malpractice claims closed against New York
physicians were closed with no expense to the insurers. By 1984, this
number had decreased slightly to 30 percent. The percentage of claims
closed with an indemnity remained fairly constant during this period at
about 30 percent, but the percentage of claims closed with cost only to
investigate and defend the claim increased from 35 to 40 percent.

Hospitals

Cost of Malpractice Insurance

As shown in table 3, the total estimated malpractice insurance costs for hospitals in New York[6] increased from $74.3 million in policy year 1983 to $96.7 million in policy year 1985—an increase of 30 percent.

Table 3: Estimated Hospital Malpractice Insurance Costs by Type of Expenditure, 1983-85

Dollars in millions

Expenditure	1983	1984	1985	1983-85 change[a] Amount	Percent
Total	$74.3	$72.9	$96.7	$22.4	30
Contributions to self-insurance trust funds	20.5	14.9	16.5	(4.0)	(20)
Premiums for purchased insurance	49.3	56.7	76.6	27.3	55
Uninsured losses	4.5	1.2	3.5	(1.0)	(22)

[a]Sampling errors for the amount and percentage of change are not presented in appendix IV, but they are comparable to the errors for the estimated costs.

Note: Detail may not add to total due to independent estimation.

As shown in table 4 for 1985, 55 percent of the hospitals had annual malpractice insurance costs of less $250,000, but 13 percent had annual costs of $1 million or more. No New York hospitals had annual costs less than $10,000 in 1983 or 1985.

---

[6]See GAO/HRD-87-21, p. 11, for methodology for obtaining and analyzing hospital cost data. See appendix III of this report for information on the number of New York hospitals in the universe, GAO's sample, and the survey response. Unless otherwise indicated, the estimates presented in this study are also included with sampling errors in tables IV.1 through IV.5.

Table 4: Estimated Distribution of Annual Malpractice Insurance Costs for Hospitals, 1983 and 1985

Annual costs	1983			1985		
	Number	Percent	Cum. percent	Number	Percent	Cum. percent
Less than 10,000	0	0	0.0	0	0.0	0
$10,000 to $24,999	10	5.6	5.6	6	3.3	3.3
$25,000 to $49,999	32	17.9	23.5	26	14.6	17.9
$50,000 to $99,999	30	16.9	40.4	22	12.4	30.3
$100,000 to $249,999	37	20.7	61.1	45	24.6	54.9
$250,000 to $499,999	27	15.3	76.4	28	15.6	70.5
$500,000 to $999,999	22	12.5	88.9	30	16.4	86.9
$1 million or more	20	11.2	100.1[a]	24	13.0	99.9[a] —
Total	**178[a]**	**100.1[a]**		**181[a]**	**99.9[a]**	

[a]Detail does not add to adjusted universe or 100 percent due to independent rounding.

As shown in table 5, the estimated average malpractice insurance cost per day increased by 36 percent from 1983 to 1985. The annual per bed cost increased by 33 percent during the same period.

Table 5: Estimated Average Hospital Malpractice Insurance Costs per Inpatient Day and per Bed,[a] 1983-85

	1983	1984	1985	Increase[b] Amount	Percent
Average malpractice cost per inpatient day	$3.81	$3.80	$5.18	$1.37	
Average annual malpractice cost per bed	$1,212	$1,181	$1,609	$397	

[a]To determine the average annual malpractice cost per bed, we computed the daily occupied bed rate (the total number of inpatient days divided by 365) and increased that number by one bed for every 2,000 outpatient visits (emergency room visits were counted as outpatient visits). This number was divided into the hospital's total annual malpractice insurance cost.

[b]Sampling errors for the amount and percent of increase are not presented in appendix IV, but they are comparable to the errors for the estimated costs.

As shown in table 6, 33 percent of the hospitals had increases of less than 10 percent or decreases in inpatient day malpractice insurance costs from 1983 to 1985. Thirty-eight percent had increases from 10 to 49 percent and 29 percent had increases of 50 percent or more.

Table 6: Estimated Distribution of Changes in Malpractice Insurance Costs per Inpatient Day From 1983 to 1985

	Hospitals		
Percentage change	Number	Percent	Cum. percent
Increases of less than 10 or all decreases	58	32.9	32.9
+10 to 49	67	37.9	70.8
+50 to 99	22	12.5	83.3
+100 to 199	20	11.3	94.6
+200 to 299	6	3.5	98.1
+300 or more	3	1.9	100.0
Total	**176[a]**	**100.0**	

[a]Does not add to adjusted universe due to independent rounding.

Note: The total number of hospitals is based on the number of responding hospitals that provided data for both 1983 and 1985 so that the percent change could be calculated.

Malpractice Insurance Rates for Hospitals

As shown in table 7, the cost of insurance for hospitals insured by Hospital Underwriters Mutual Insurance Company remained unchanged from 1980 to 1985. However, from 1985 to 1986 the rate increased 32 percent.

Table 7: Rates[a] per Occupied Bed for Primary Coverage, 1980-86

Territory[b]	Policy type	1980	1983	1985	1986
1	Claims-made	[c]	$479.10	$479.10	$632.00
1	Occurrence	$504.32	504.32	504.32	664.00
2	Claims-made	[c]	366.81	366.81	483.00
2	Occurrence	386.12	386.12	386.12	508.00

[a]Rates shown are those of the Hospital Underwriters Mutual Insurance Company for $1 million/$3 million occurrence and claims-made policies.

[b]Territory 1 = New York City area; Territory 2 = remainder of state.

[c]Data not available.

Frequency of Claims

The combined claims experience for insurers of New York hospitals indicated that the frequency of claims filed per 100 occupied beds increased from 1980 to 1984. As shown in figure 3, the frequency of claims filed against hospitals increased from 7.5 in 1980 to 8.7 in 1984—16 percent.

Figure 3: Frequency of Claims per 100 Occupied Hospital Beds, 1980-84

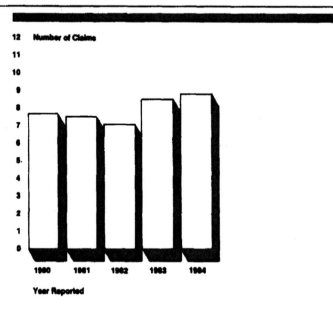

Size of Awards and Settlements

As shown in figure 4, from 1980 to 1984 the average paid claim against New York hospitals remained relatively unchanged.

Figure 4: Average Paid Claim for Hospitals, 1980-84

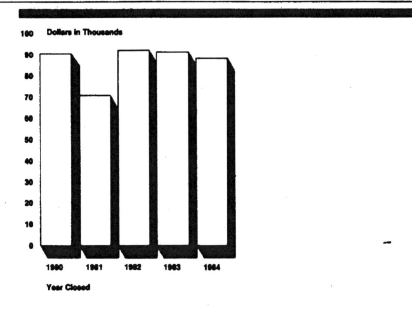

Cost to Investigate and Defend Claims

Combined data from New York insurers show that the average cost to investigate and defend claims against New York hospitals increased from $4,922 in 1980 to $8,900 in 1984—an increase of 81 percent.

From 1980 to 1984, the percentage of malpractice claims closed against New York hospitals with no expense to the insurers decreased from 45 to 35 percent; however, also over this period, the percent of claims closed with payment to the claimant increased from 25 to 31 percent, and the percentage closed with cost only to investigate and defend the claim increased from 30 to 33 percent.

Major Medical Malpractice Problems—Current and Future

Major current or future malpractice problems in New York identified by three or more of the interest groups[7] we surveyed related to the

- length of time to resolve medical malpractice claims,
- cost of medical malpractice liability insurance,
- individual physician actions to reduce or prevent medical malpractice claims,
- availability of medical malpractice liability insurance,
- number of medical malpractice claims filed,
- size of awards/settlements for medical malpractice claims, and
- legal expenses/attorney's fees for medical malpractice claims.

Length of Time to Resolve Malpractice Claims

A major current or future concern identified by three or more of the six interest groups concerned the long time required to resolve medical malpractice claims.

The New York Hospital Association stated that it takes an average of 8 years for a malpractice case to be settled in New York State, which clearly adds to the costs of the system for all parties.

The New York Bar Association stated that the difficulty in obtaining physicians' depositions, together with a requirement for panel screening of cases, greatly and unnecessarily increases the length of time to resolve claims.

The New York Trial Lawyers Association also believed that the delays have been exacerbated by medical malpractice panel hearings, which virtually were a second trial that must be held before the real trial can take place.

The Hospital Underwriters Association stated that: "All time frames - court delays (including panel) are outrageous in New York. Patients without other resources are in trouble financially and emotionally."

The physician group felt that the long time to resolve claims put an emotional burden on them. The trial lawyers association felt the emotional burden was on the injured patient.

---

[7]Our methodology for obtaining the views of major interest groups and for analyzing their responses is described in GAO/HRD-87-21, pp. 10-11. The specific interest groups for New York are presented in appendix II of this report.

Cost of Malpractice Insurance

The cost of medical malpractice insurance was thought to be too expensive by five of the six interest groups surveyed. The physician group, hospital association, trial lawyers association, malpractice insurers, and insurance department believed that the cost of basic liability coverage for physicians was too expensive. These same groups also believed that the cost of basic liability coverage for hospitals was too expensive. In addition, the malpractice insurer group and the insurance department believed that the current cost of excess liability coverage was too expensive for both physicians and hospitals and that this problem would continue in future years.

The malpractice insurer group felt that the cost of reinsurance was too expensive currently and would be in the future and that "tail" coverage[8] would be a problem in future years. The leading insurer of physicians stated that the excessive cost was caused by the frequency and severity of awards and expressed concern that rates will continue to be a very substantial problem for providers over the next 5 years without significant legislative action.

Individual Physicians' Actions to Reduce or Prevent Medical Malpractice Claims

The physician group and malpractice insurers believed that physicians have strong incentives to perform medically unnecessary tests or treatments to reduce their risk of liability.

The Medical Malpractice Insurance Association indicated that the frequency of suits and judgments has made physicians defensive and self-protective. Still another insurer, Merson and Company, indicated that very few physicians take the time to explain procedures and problems to patients. The leading physician insurer, Medical Liability Mutual Insurance Company, stated that:

" 'Defensive Medicine' has increasingly become a serious problem - while some actions may be nothing more than good medical practice, there are undoubtedly unnecessary tests, x-rays, etc., which are performed solely to protect the physician from liability exposure. Further, there is a tendency to shy away from more aggressive approaches when needed because of liability exposure."

The New York State Academy of Family Physicians indicated that physicians are trying to "second guess" possible problems to be sure that anything that might be asked for is charted to show that they did indeed

---

[8]A claims-made policy covers malpractice events that occur after the effective date of the coverage and for which claims are made during the policy period. Insurance to cover claims filed after the claims-made policy has expired is known as "tail" coverage.

think of that test or diagnosis and they are placing less reliance on professional opinion, which makes for a bad patient care relationship.

Availability of Malpractice Insurance

The availability of basic liability coverage was not perceived as a major problem in New York, as indicated by the response of all six of the groups we surveyed. However, four of the six groups indicated that physicians were unable to find a source for desired levels of excess liability coverage. The physician group and the malpractice insurer group believed that the lack of available excess coverage and the inability to find sufficient levels of reinsurance were current problems that would continue in future years.

Since our survey was conducted, New York passed legislation in 1985 which now makes available excess liability coverage for physicians. However, according to the New York Hospital Association,

"hospitals are facing an acute problem of purchasing excess insurance as it is not available or it is available at 300 - 400 [percent] increase over prior years. The excess insurance market is drying up."

According to the Medical Malpractice Insurance Association, the "insurance market appears to be unwilling to provide excess and reinsurance coverages on an occurrence basis. [The] Market is very tight and will probably become tighter."

Also, according to the Medical Liability Mutual Insurance Company, ". . . These problems [are] due to insurer concern about severity of awards."

According to one hospital insurer, the Federation of Jewish Philanthropies Service Corporation, "obtaining reinsurance is a substantial problem for insurers and will be a very great problem in the future because of its limited market."

The Hospital Underwriters Mutual Insurance Company (HUM) stated that:

"Either it [reinsurance] is not available or too expensive. Since 1983, HUM has had no reinsurance because it is too expensive and because no companies wanted to reinsure HUM at even a somewhat reasonable rate. The large hospitals in New York city are self-insured or not insured because they simply cannot find reinsurance."

Number of Malpractice Claims Filed

Four of the six groups surveyed indicated that they were concerned over the large number of frivolous claims. The physician group, malpractice insurers, and the trial lawyers association believed that the large number of frivolous claims was currently a problem and would continue to be a problem in the future.

The New York Hospital Association commented that it is difficult to try to quantify the impact of frivolous claims as well as the basis for the large number of frivolous claims. However, since 57 percent of the cases are dropped with no compensation being awarded, many of the cases must be of a frivolous nature. The association added that even though these cases are dropped, there are still inherent court costs that have a great effect on the system. The association commented that many insurers are encouraged to settle out of court even in frivolous cases. The leading insurer of physicians, the Medical Liability Mutual Insurance Company, stated that the

"Company closes more than half of all lawsuits without any indemnity indicating substantial number of cases without merit. Public expectations of perfect results of treatment have produced many claims. Also publicity and advertisements about large awards have whetted appetites of litigants . . . Reported claims at present, represent a tiny fraction of patient encounters."

Size of Awards and Settlements for Malpractice Claims

All of the physician organizations surveyed believed that awards/settlements were excessive in relation to economic costs arising from the injuries and for pain and suffering and were a major problem currently and would be in future years. Also, with the exception of one physician organization, the physician group agreed that too many awards/settlements over $1 million was a current major problem and all physicians' organizations agreed it would be so in future years. The hospital association also believed that they were current problems. The malpractice insurer group also believed major current and future problems were that awards/settlements and amounts paid for pain and suffering were excessive and that there were too many $1 million payments. The New York State Academy of Family Physicians stated that:

"Amounts that are being used for purposes of suit have escalated dramatically to the point where the sky is the limit. This causes a need for increased amount of insurance reserves creating escalating insurance cost which are becoming impossible to meet."

The Medical Liability Mutual Insurance Company stated:

"Severity has increased dramatically. Average awards increased from $36,000 in 1976 to $134,000 in 1984. Million dollar verdicts were non existent in New York State in 1975. From January 1984 - May 1985 [the] Company was involved in 15 jury verdicts in excess of 1 million dollars."

The Federation of Jewish Philanthropies Service Corporation believed that awards/settlements were excessive in relation to the economic costs arising from the injuries and for pain and suffering because of sympathy for the injured patient. They also stated that:

". . . too many awards in excess of one million dollars [were] not only because of the subjectivity of the jury system but because awards of such amounts have been made more public via newspapers, television, etc. Thus, such amounts have become 'expected' in the minds of the jurors."

Legal Expenses and Attorney's Fees for Malpractice Claims

Four of the six groups surveyed indicated that legal expenses, and attorney's fees, as a percentage of awards/settlements are too high. The physician group and malpractice insurers, and the trial lawyers association believed that this was a problem that would continue in the future. The hospital association believed it was currently a problem. The Medical Liability Mutual Insurance Company stated that:

"Legal costs for both sides equal or may even slightly exceed the dollars paid to the claimant to compensate for injury - Plaintiff's contingency fee has been around 33 1/3 [percent] of recovery (modestly reduced by recent statute) Defense fees estimated to be between 15 - 20 [percent]. Plaintiffs contingency fees impede prompt disposition of cases."

A representative of the Medical Society of the State of New York stated that "a system for quickly settling claims may provide the injured party a greater portion of the award because it will reduce legal costs of both parties."

The American College of Obstetricians and Gynecologists, District II felt that "Legal fees, both defense and plaintiff, consume the bulk of malpractice premiums, rather than them going to injured patients."

Solutions to Malpractice Problems

State action to strengthen licensing and relicensing for physicians was the most widely supported action among the six groups we surveyed in New York. The New York Hospital Association stated that "Steps, in regards to licensing of physicians, have been taken to deal with foreign doctors, but more needs to be done overall." An official of the New York Bar Association stated that in the area of the medical profession policing themselves he questioned whether there is any medical policing occurring in the profession. He added that rating physicians on their experience by looking at their claims and actual losses is a better method of policing the profession rather than through license revoking.

Role of the Federal Government

Of the six groups surveyed in New York, the physician group was the only one to support any form of federal intervention in the state. This group indicated that a uniform system for resolving medical malpractice claims should be mandated by the federal government. The Medical Society of the State of New York stated that at first it was not in favor of federal intervention; however, New York has been unable to solve its medical malpractice problems, so the society now is more in favor of some type of federal intervention.

The New York Hospital Association, bar association, trial lawyers association, malpractice insurers, and the insurance department all expressed a desire for the federal government to not be involved in the state medical malpractice problem.

Medical Malpractice Insurers Requested to Provide Statistical Data for New York

	Provided data for		Did not provide requested data
	Physicians	Hospitals	
Affiliated Risk Control Administrators, Inc.	X	X	
The CIGNA Group			X
Federation of Jewish Philanthropies Service Corporation	X	X	
Hospital Underwriters Mutual Insurance Company		X	
Medical Malpractice Insurance Association	X		
Medical Liability Mutual Insurance Company	X	X	
Medical Quadrangle, Incorporated	X		
Merson and Company	X[b]	X[b]	
New York City Health and Hospital Corporation		X[a]	
Physicians' Reciprocal Insurers			X
St. Paul Fire & Marine Insurance Company		X	

[a]Data not included in our data base due to several missing data elements.

[b]Data not included in our data base because it would duplicate data from Affiliated Risk Control Administrators, Inc.

Organizations Receiving GAO Questionnaire for New York

Completing questionnaire	Not completing questionnaire
Physician group:	
Medical Society of the State of New York	New York State Society of Pathologists
The American College of Obstetricians and	New York State Opthalmological Society
Gynecologists, District II	New York Regional Society of Plastic and Reconstructive Surgery
New York State Society of Anesthesiologists	
New York State Neurosurgical Society, Inc.	New York State Psychiatric Association, Inc.
District II, American Academy of Pediatrics	New York State Chapter, American College of Radiology
Nassau County Medical Center - Acting Chairman of Pediatrics	
New York State Academy of Family Physicians	
New York State Society of Orthopaedic Surgeons, Inc.	
New York State Society of Surgeons, Inc.	
Hospital association:	
New York Hospital Association	
Bar association:	
New York Bar Association	
Trial lawyers:	
New York State Trial Lawyers Association	
Malpractice insurers:	
Medical Liability Mutual Insurance Company	St. Paul Fire and Marine Insurance Company
Hospital Underwriters Mutual Insurance Company	The CIGNA Group
Federation of Jewish Philanthropies Service Corporation	
Merson and Company	
Affiliated Risk Control Administrators, Inc.	
Medical Malpractice Insurance Association	
New York City Health and Hospitals Corporation	
Medical Quadrangle, Inc.	
Physicians Reciprocal Insurers	
Insurance department:	
State of New York Insurance Department	

Number of New York Hospitals in the Universe, GAO Sample, and Survey Response

Number of hospitals		Hospitals completing questionnaire	
Universe[a]	Sample	Number	Percent
267	151	111	74

[a]1983 data.

Estimated Hospital Data and Related Sampling Errors for Policy Years 1983, 1984, and 1985

Table IV.1: Hospital Malpractice Insurance Costs and Related Sampling Errors by Type of Expenditure

Dollars in Millions

	1983		1984		1985	
Expenditure	Amount	Sampling error[a]	Amount	Sampling error[a]	Amount	Sampling error[a]
Total costs	$74.3	$7.4	$72.9	$6.4	$96.7	$9.5
Contributions to self-insurance trust funds	20.5	5.4	14.9	4.1	16.5	4.7
Premiums for purchased insurance	49.3	6.8	56.7	7.1	76.6	9.6
Uninsured losses	4.5	3.5	1.2	.6	3.5	2.6

[a]Sampling errors are stated at the 95-percent confidence level.

Note: Detail may not add to total due to independent estimation. The adjusted universe of hospitals to which the estimated amounts relate were 177 in 1983 and 182 in 1984 and 1985. The adjusted universe is that portion of the total universe based on the sample response rate for which we can estimate data.

Table IV.2: Distribution of Annual Malpractice Insurance Costs and Related Sampling Errors for Hospitals

Figures in percents

	1983		1985	
Annual cost	Hospitals	Sampling error[a]	Hospitals	Sampling error[a]
Less than $10,000	0.0	0.0	0.0	0.0
$10,000 to $24,999	5.6	3.0	3.3	2.4
$25,000 to $49,999	17.9	4.6	14.6	4.6
$50,000 to $99,999	16.9	5.5	12.4	4.7
$100,000 to $249,999	20.7	5.6	24.6	5.8
$250,000 to $499,999	15.3	4.3	15.6	4.4
$500,000 to $999,999	12.5	3.6	16.4	3.4
$1 million or more	11.2	2.4	13.0	2.5

[a]Sampling errors are stated at the 95-percent confidence level.

Note: The adjusted universe of hospitals was 177 in 1983 and 182 in 1985.

Table IV.3: Average Malpractice Insurance Costs Per Inpatient Day and Related Sampling Errors

1983		1984		1985	
Cost per day	Sampling error[a]	Cost per day	Sampling error[a]	Cost per day	Sampling error[a]
$3.81	$0.35	$3.80	$0.33	$5.18	$0.57

[a]Sampling errors are stated at the 95-percent confidence level.

Table IV.4: Average Annual Malpractice Insurance Costs per Bed and Related Sampling Errors

1983		1984		1985	
Cost per bed	Sampling error[a]	Cost per bed	Sampling error[a]	Cost per bed	Sampling error[a]
$1,212	$118	$1,181	$110	$1,609	$171

[a]Sampling errors are stated at the 95-percent confidence level.

Table IV.5: Distribution of Changes in Malpractice Insurance Costs per Inpatient Day From 1983 to 1985 and Related Sampling Errors

Figures in percents

Changes	Hospitals	Sampling error[a]
Increases of less than 10% or decreases	32.9	6.6
Increases of 10% to 49%	37.9	6.6
Increases of 50% to 99%	12.5	3.7
Increases of 100% to 199%	11.3	4.6
Increases of 200% to 299%	3.5	2.2
Increases of 300% or more	1.9	1.7

[a]Sampling errors are stated at the 95-percent confidence level.

Note: The adjusted universe of hospitals was 177.

United States
General Accounting Office
Washington, D.C. 20548

Official Business
Penalty for Private Use $300

Address Correction Requested

CPSIA information can be obtained at www.ICGtesting.com
Printed in the USA
BVOW07s2305130514

353460BV00007B/238/P